# Fiji Facts and Figures

Written by Claire Owen

My name is Joeli. I live in beautiful Fiji. Would you like to visit a Pacific Island? How would you get there? What do you think the weather would be like?

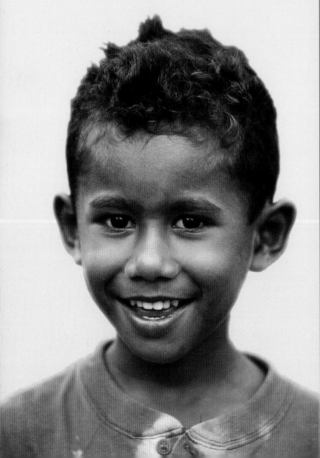

# Contents

Wherever you see me, you'll find activities to try and questions to answer.

# Fabulous Fiji

Fiji is an archipelago (AR kuh PEL uh go) in the Pacific Ocean. It has 322 islands that are large enough for people to live on, but only 106 islands actually have people living on them. Fiji has a population of more than 800,000 people. Almost nine-tenths of Fijians live on the two largest islands.

Viti Levu, the main island of Fiji, is home to seven-tenths of the population.

archipelago   a large body of water with many islands

Fiji is a popular place for vacations. There are direct flights to Fiji from New Zealand and other countries around the rim of the Pacific Ocean.

## Distances from Fiji (Miles)

CANADA

Vancouver

JAPAN

Tokyo

UNITED STATES OF AMERICA

Los Angeles

5,871

Honolulu

5,524

4,428

3,166

With a partner, take turns picking a distance on the map and reading it aloud. Then write the distances in order, from least to greatest.

FIJI

AUSTRALIA

Sydney

1,961

2,395

1,328

Melbourne

Auckland

NEW ZEALAND

# Cloth from Bark

The people of the Pacific have been making cloth from the bark of the paper mulberry tree for hundreds of years. In Fiji, this bark cloth is called *masi*. In other parts of the Pacific, it is known as *tapa*. It is a tradition in Fiji to wear masi cloth at weddings and on other special occasions. Newborn babies are often wrapped in masi, too.

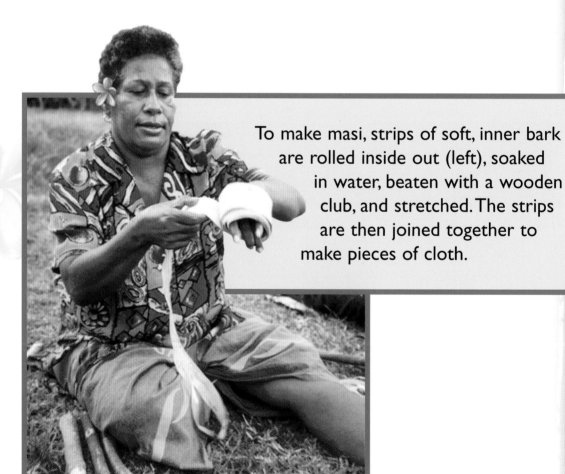

To make masi, strips of soft, inner bark are rolled inside out (left), soaked in water, beaten with a wooden club, and stretched. The strips are then joined together to make pieces of cloth.

tradition   an old and special way of doing things

Women use stencils made from banana leaves or clear plastic to decorate the white masi with black and brown patterns.

# Did You Know?

A right-angle triangle has one angle that looks like a square corner.

An equilateral triangle has three equal sides and three equal angles.

An isosceles triangle has two equal sides and two equal angles.

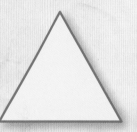

In the design at the left, can you find a right-angle triangle ... an equilateral triangle ... an isosceles triangle ... an isosceles triangle that has a right angle?

# Tropical Temperatures

Fiji has a mild tropical climate. During the day, the maximum temperature is usually between 80 and 90 degrees Fahrenheit. Even at night, the temperature is around 70 degrees Fahrenheit. Fiji is a great place for swimming and snorkeling, because the water temperature is usually around 80 degrees!

maximum   the highest measurement that has been reached

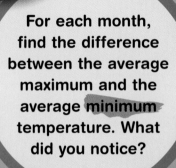

For each month, find the difference between the average maximum and the average minimum temperature. What did you notice?

| Temperatures (°F) (Suva, Fiji) | | |
|---|---|---|
| Month | Average Maximum | Average Minimum |
| January | 86 | 74 |
| February | 86 | 74 |
| March | 86 | 74 |
| April | 84 | 73 |
| May | 82 | 71 |
| June | 80 | 69 |
| July | 79 | 68 |
| August | 79 | 68 |
| September | 80 | 69 |
| October | 81 | 70 |
| November | 83 | 71 |
| December | 85 | 73 |

**minimum** the lowest measurement that has been reached

# Rainfall Facts

In Fiji, the wet season lasts from December to April. During this time, the weather is hot and humid, and there may be a heavy shower of rain in the late afternoon. The dry season is from May to November. Some parts of Fiji get very little rain during this season. However, some places, such as Suva, have rain all year round.

humid    when the air is full of water vapor; damp

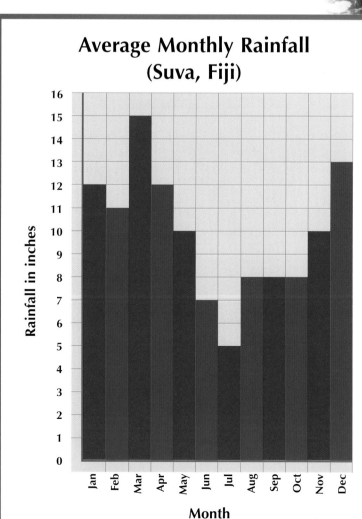

**Average Monthly Rainfall (Suva, Fiji)**

Rainfall in inches

Month

Bouma Waterfall, Fiji

# Figure It Out

Use the data in
the bar graph to
solve these problems.

1. In Suva, which month is—
   a. the wettest?
   b. the driest?

2. How many months have—
   a. less than 9 inches of rain?
   b. 12 inches of rain or more?

3. What is the total rainfall in—
   a. the wet season?
   b. the dry season?

4. What is the average annual
   rainfall for Suva?

5. How much more rain falls
   in March than in—
   a. April?          c. June?
   b. December?       d. August?

6. How much more rain falls
   in the wettest month than
   in the driest month?

annual   for a period of a year;
         each year

# Rainy Days

In tropical countries, rainstorms can be very heavy, but they often do not last long. Other places might get the same amount of rain, but it is spread over a longer time. To help give people a better understanding of the weather, meteorologists count the days each month on which rain falls. The chart below shows this information for Suva.

| Average Number of Rainy Days (Suva, Fiji) | | | | | | | | | | | |
|---|---|---|---|---|---|---|---|---|---|---|---|
| Jan | Feb | Mar | Apr | May | Jun | Jul | Aug | Sep | Oct | Nov | Dec |
| 18 | 18 | 21 | 19 | 16 | 13 | 14 | 15 | 16 | 15 | 15 | 18 |

meteorologist  a scientist who studies the weather and makes forecasts

# Make a Bar Graph

To make a bar graph that shows the number
of rainy days for Suva, you will need a sheet of grid paper.

---

**1.** Write a title for the graph at the
top of the grid paper.

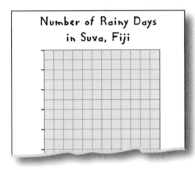

**2.** Number every row or
second row, starting with 0
at the bottom of the grid.

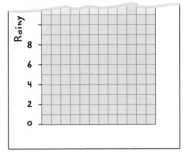

---

**3.** Write "J" for January below the
first column. Color squares to
show 18 rainy days.

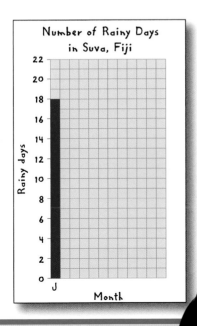

**4.** Continue with "F" for
February, "M" for March,
and so on.

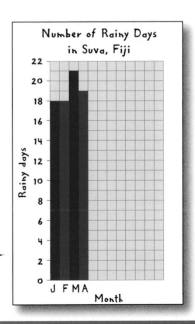

# Cruising the Pacific

More than 400,000 people visit Fiji each year. Most of these visitors arrive by air, but about 8,000 come by sea. Some of the sailors who visit Fiji are traveling around the world! Others are "island hopping" around the Pacific Ocean.

How far is it from Fiji to the Solomon Islands, via Vanuatu? From Fiji, how much farther is it to New Caledonia than to Vanuatu?

SOLOMON ISLANDS

SAMOA

738

VANUATU    501    FIJI

280                     712

660                          485

468

NEW CALEDONIA

855                     TONGA

NORFOLK ISLAND

Make up an addition problem and a subtraction problem for a partner to solve. (Use distances from the map in your problems.)

## Did You Know?

Distances at sea are measured in nautical miles. (A nautical mile is about 2,026 yards long.) The speed of a boat is measured in knots. One knot is one nautical mile per hour.

via  by way of

# Sample Answers

Choose another Pacific country, such as Vanuatu or New Caledonia. Find out some facts and figures about that country.

**Page 5**    Distances (miles):
1,328; 1,961; 2,395; 3,166;
4,428; 5,524; 5,871

**Page 9**    Differences (degrees):
12, 12, 12, 11, 11, 11, 11, 11, 11,
11, 12, 12 (All differences are
11 or 12 degrees.)

**Page 11**
1.  a. March        b. July
2.  a. 5 months     b. 4 months
3.  a. 63 inches    b. 56 inches
4.  119 inches
5.  a. 3 inches     c. 8 inches
    b. 2 inches     d. 7 inches
6.  10 inches

**Page 15**    1,239 miles; 159 miles

# Index